MW00413195

A Passion for Monday

Love Monday, Just Like Friday, but for a Different Reason

Ryan Houmand

ISBN: 1518688195
ISBN-13: 978-1518688195

DEDICATION

To my dad who was the first person to every tell me I can make it in this world if I do what I love. Dad, you were right!

CONTENTS

	Introduction	1
1	Why Do We Hate Monday?	6
2	Reasons We Hate Monday: Lacking Skills	9
3	Reasons We Hate Monday: Lacking Talent	12
4	Reasons We Hate Monday: Unmet Needs	15
5	3 Mistakes that Make People Hate Monday	19
6	Mistake #1: The Michael Jordan Mistake	21
7	Mistake #2: The Marty McFly Mistake	23
8	Mistake #3: The Caitlyn Jenner Mistake	27
9	My Story: A Particularly Hateful Monday	31
10	Play to Your Strengths	48
11	Stop Trying to Be Well-Rounded	52
12	Don't Live Someone Else's Dream	56
13	Finding a Passion for Monday	58

ACKNOWLEDGMENTS

I'm grateful to all who have supported me in my dream to change the world of work and help people LOVE Monday, just like Friday, but for a different reason. I've drawn upon a lot of the research of others and pulled a lot of inspiration from observing a lot of people who are famously successful at what they do, some of whom you'll read about in this book. I hope you'll find your own passion for Monday.

INTRODUCTION
WHEN DOES MONDAY START?

When does Monday arrive for you? It sounds like a ridiculous question because common sense would tell you it arrives whenever you wake on Monday morning. But think about it. When do you start to feel dread about what you're facing on Monday? Is it at 9:00 PM on Sunday night? Earlier? Does your Monday start at noon on Sunday? Whatever the time, if Monday comes before you rise on Monday, you're probably not happy in your job. You're certainly not engaged.

According to Gallup, only 30% of workers are engaged at work. That means 7 out of 10 people HATE Monday. Also, according to Gallup, an engaged employee is involved in, enthusiastic about, and committed to their work and contribute to their organization in a positive way. If, for you, Monday arrives before Monday morning, you're part of the 70%. Your career shouldn't be a source of dread. If it is, you're doing something wrong.

I want you to be part of the 3 and not the 7. The thinking that went into this book is all about that.

I spent the better part of 20 years as a manager in a large corporation. The part of my job that I loved the most was hiring great people and helping them further their careers. Most often, the people I hired or managed, furthered their careers within the company, but sometimes it was best for them, based on their strengths to go elsewhere. I recall an interview with an internal candidate who was looking for a promotion to a position that was posted on one of my teams. During the interview I noticed that some of the examples he used to highlight his successes were highly energizing to him. I asked him more questions about the particular job from which those energetic examples came. I found that he could go on and on about that job. He told me in detail about the work environment, the job itself, and the success he and his team enjoyed. In the end, he was not the best fit for the job for which he was interviewing. He had been at the company for several years and was struggling to get into a role that he really wanted. He wanted to make more money, but that seemed to be his main motivation. He was overlooking something that was obvious to me – he didn't have any passion for any of the jobs for which he had been applying. He didn't have passion for them, because they probably didn't require what he did best. They did not allow him to use his talent. As I did with all internal applicants, I offered him an opportunity to set up time with me, at his leisure, if he wanted feedback on why he didn't get the job. Interestingly, only a fraction of the people I offered this to, ever took me up on it. To his credit, he set up time to meet with me. I gave him feedback on the logistics of the interview, things he did well, things he didn't do so well. Next, I told him that most of all, he didn't seem to be a good fit for the job. It didn't seem to match his abilities very well. Finally, I told him that I thought he should try find a job like the one he had described in the interview. Possibly even go back to the place where he had all that passion and energy, or even somewhere else where he could recapture that enthusiasm. Someplace where he could play to his greatest strengths.

That's what it's about. Playing to your strengths. It's the only way to be truly successful. If you have thought all your life that trying to turn your weaknesses into strengths is the way to success, I respectfully submit that you're wrong. It's not your fault. That's the conventional wisdom and society underscores that focusing on your weaknesses is the way to self-improvement. We want to be well-rounded. And by well-rounded we generally mean good at everything, or at least lots of things. You cannot excel where you are strong if you insist on being good at things for which you have no talent. Even if it were possible, consider the cost you incur in terms of your undeveloped strengths. For every hour spent working on your weaknesses, it's an hour lost on developing your strengths. In fact, the cost is a lot greater than that. Focusing on your strengths will give you *exponential* improvement. Focusing on your weaknesses yields only a *logarithmic* improvement, at best. With exponential growth, you improve at an increasing rate over time. With logarithmic growth, you will experience early growth based on new information, but that growth quickly trails off to little improvement regardless of the amount of time spent. The bottom line is, the cost at being good at lots of things is that you won't be great or superb or world-class at anything.

I want you to discover and play to your strengths. When you do, you will develop a passion for Monday.

You don't have to be a part of the 70% of

workers who hate Monday. It's possible for you to love Monday, just like Friday, but for a different reason.

1

WHY DO WE HATE MONDAY?

You don't have to hate Monday, you know? If you already do, chances are you have hated Monday for a while now. You might think it's just the way life is. Work is work, it's not supposed to be fun, right? That it's called work, and that it feels like work is no coincidence. But if you're thinking that Mondays are hateful and everybody feels this way, you're wrong. We already established this with that Gallup statistic about employee engagement. We said only 30% of workers are engaged at work, remember? But that's the point, 30% *are* engaged at work. If you're thinking that they are engaged at work because they work someplace where there's free soda and unlimited time off and a ping-pong table, you're wrong. There are lots of people that work at places with all that and are still part of the 70%. The people in the 30% are doing something differently. And what they're doing makes it so they don't hate Mondays. You can get there too!

Now that we know there's hope, let's look at why we hate Monday in more detail.

We hate Monday because of stress related

to our work. The Centers for Disease Control (CDC) tell us that "job stress results when the requirements of the job do not match the capabilities, needs or resources of the worker." In effect, we are not getting opportunities to do what we do best every day because we lack the skills and/or talent and our needs are not met by the job.

3 Reasons We Hate Monday

2

REASONS WE HATE MONDAY

REASON #1: LACKING SKILLS

You applied for the job, and your employer hired you, so at least at that point in time you were viewed as having the skills for the job. Now, for whatever reason, your skills do not match the requirements of the job and you feel you are in over your head. Perhaps, there was a reorganization and now you find yourself in a different position, one for which you did not apply, but regardless you are in a new seat on the bus, and the seat is hard and uncomfortable.

You dread every day because you're not sure how you're going to get through another one. Maybe the requirements of the job have changed since you were hired. When people feel they lack the skills, or no longer have the skills for the job, one or more of the following has happened:

1. There wasn't a proper assessment and matching of employee skills with job requirements
2. Training was insufficient or not understood

3. The employee is still new and has not had enough time to learn all the skills required for proper execution of the job.

The good news is that all three of these items are easily corrected. The bad news is, skills alone are not enough to make you love Monday like Friday, but we'll explore that later. If your skills were not properly matched for the new job, that's in the past and with enough training you can learn the skills to be competent in this new role.

If you have not been properly trained, you can have a discussion with your immediate supervisor. That conversation can go something like this:

"You may not have noticed, but I'm not comfortable with my ability to perform my job. I want to do my job well and be a top performer. I simply don't understand all the tasks I have to perform. Specifically, I am having trouble in these areas…"

I've was a manager in a large organization for many years, trust me when I say, if every time someone was struggling with their job, they had come to me first, it would have made everything a lot easier for both of us. You're manager will appreciate your candor and your willingness to do a great job. Only a bad manager would look down on you for admitting weakness. If that's the case, you don't want to work for that manager anyway, so even if the worst should happen, you're better off.

If you simply haven't had enough time to learn the new skills, just give it time. Observe others who seem to have mastered the job. Go to them for advice, ask them for their tips and tricks. Imagine if the tables were turned and someone came to you and said:

"I've noticed you do a really great job here, and I'm hoping to be as good at this job as you are someday. However, I have to admit I'm struggling. Would you be willing to share what you do to be so successful in doing…?"

Can you imagine not helping someone who said that to you? What's more, can you imagine not having a stronger connection with that person after expressing so much trust in you? Of course, you would help them! And you're likely to bore them with way more information than they need, because you're ecstatic that someone finally noticed the great work you do! Seek help from the best of the best where you work, you'll be amazed at the things you'll learn and the friendships you build.

3

REASONS WE HATE MONDAY
REASON #2: LACKING TALENT

Lacking talent. Those two words bring discomfort, and for good reason. We don't want to think we lack talent. We don't want to be viewed as less than anyone else, because we are conditioned to look at work and life as a bit of a competition. If you're doing better than me, you will get all the rewards, recognition and opportunities. If you're more talented than me I'm going to miss out, and so we compete and try to be like someone else. We're conditioned this way because for a very long time now, this is exactly what has been happening in the workplace. We see one of our peers who seems to be so good at the same job at which we are struggling. We analyze the situation with frustration because "I used to be so good" and "I've always been a top performer" and "I've won awards and been recognized as the expert, and the 'go-to' and one who delivers excellent service". You wonder why you are struggling. You wonder if you're losing your edge. You worry that people are getting better than you, and you are actually getting worse. Perhaps you worry that you're losing your ability to learn. Maybe you think with age you are less able to learn and adapt than you used to be. You're career airplane has stalled and you're falling into a tail-spinning death spiral.

Time out!

Before you crash and burn, remember, what changed here - the job, not you. You're the same person you always were. If you once felt you were rockin' it, then you've changed jobs, or the job changed on you. And for the record, studies have shown that your ability to learn is not reduced until you are well into your 70s and then only in a small degree. No, you're not losing your edge due to age. That's not even possible.

For now, it is enough to know that back then, when you experienced rapid learning, were energized and seemed to automatically know the things you needed to be do, you probably loved Mondays. The people you see around you that love Mondays are experiencing those things now. The difference is, the job they are doing draws upon and feeds their talents. Meanwhile, you are picking up the skills, but you don't love the job and you're not sure you ever will. I will level with you, if you don't possess the talents to really thrive in this job, you probably never will like it. You will go on hating Monday. Sorry to be the bearer of bad news, but it's better that you find out sooner than later so that you can move on to that job you can rock!

If you don't have the talent to be able to thrive, you are likely to struggle regardless of the amount of training, time on job and other support you receive. That's not to say, you can't learn the skills to be competent, but talent is not over-rated. If you are in a job for which your specific set of talents does not fit the job, it will likely always cause a sort of internal friction for you. Why? Because unlike that peer to whom you are comparing yourself, it doesn't come easily for you. You don't derive energy from it. Time doesn't pass without notice. Because that peer has in-born talent for this job, you will always feel you are under-preforming by comparison. If you truly lack the talents required for the job, you will never perform it at the level that the star performer you're comparing yourself to, performs it. As disheartening as that sounds, changing jobs to one which feeds your talent is a good thing, not a bad thing.

4

REASONS WE HATE MONDAY
REASON #3: UNMET NEEDS

If your needs are not met by the job, you will also have work-related stress and you will hate Mondays. What do we mean by needs? Talent is part of this. If the job does not allow you the opportunity to do what you do best every day, that is a very basic need. You will always yearn to do what you do best, but be starved for opportunities.

Another area of unmet needs is in your vision and values. If you do not share the vision and values of your organization, you probably will never feel this job is a good fit for you. For example, if your particular set of values pushes you to be environmentally conscious, but you are working for a highly polluting and environmentally destructive organization, you will never feel good about working there. You will never be able to get behind what the organization is trying to do. If the values of your organization are not aligned with yours, you probably will have to move to a new organization. Most often, we discover ourselves in a bad organizational fit, not because the organization changed, but because we didn't do our homework when we applied for the job. Most people, when looking for a job, take the shotgun approach and send as many resumes to as many companies who have all the jobs that match their skills. We seldom look at things like the mission, vision and values of the company and really think about whether or not we are aligned with the organization. So now, if you find you need to change to a place where your values and vision are more aligned, you're better off finding 1-3 organizations at most, and really focus your job search efforts on those organizations.

There are some other specific areas of need, which if not met, will contribute to our contempt for Mondays. These are taken from the 12 elements of engagement scientifically proven to be the primary predictors of employee motivation. Gallup performed the biggest study of its kind which spanned decades with thousands of interviews and asking thousands of questions.

The 12 elements that emerged were:

1. I know what's expected of me at work.
2. I have the materials and equipment I need to do my job right.

3. At work I have the opportunity to do what I do best every day.
4. In the last 7 days, I have received recognition or praise for doing good work.
5. My supervisor, or someone at work, seems to care about me as a person.
6. There is someone at work who encourages my development.
7. At work, my opinions seem to count.
8. The mission or purpose of my organization makes me feel my job is important.
9. My associates or fellow employees are committed to doing quality work
10. I have a best friend at work.
11. In the last 6 months, someone at work has talked to me about my progress.
12. This last year, I have had opportunities at work to learn and grow.

If your needs are not being met in these areas, it will be difficult for you to really love Mondays, but not impossible. These factors are mentioned because even if you do all you can, to focus on your talents and doing what you do best, there may be some organizational challenges beyond your ability to control.

We may also hate Mondays due to things

we do to ourselves. These are closely related to some of the items already discussed, but these are outcomes of those sources of work stress – things we do to ourselves. I see three common mistakes that make people hate Mondays.

5

3 MISTAKES THAT MAKE PEOPLE HATE MONDAY

While there are many factors contributing to why people hate Mondays, there are 3 common mistakes that make the problem a whole lot worse. We see people making these mistakes all the time and with the best of intentions. These 3 mistakes, if avoided, will go a long way toward making Mondays good again. You might even be making some of them. I believe most people do in one form or another and to some degree or another.

These mistakes are:

1. The Michael Jordan Mistake – trying to be good at everything
2. The Marty McFly Mistake – fixating on your weaknesses
3. The Caitlyn Jenner Mistake – living someone else's dream

It is not my intent to make light of anyone's situation. These examples named for people both real and fictional shed an identifiable and relatable light on mistakes most of us make at one time or another. In all of these situations, the people involved were headed along a course initially thought to be the best. However, while on that course they felt a dissonance that made them choose a course more true to them as individuals. These people, two real, and one a character in a popular movie franchise, eventually found their truth and followed a new course. That's the true happy ending in all of this.

6

3 MISTAKES

MISTAKE #1 – THE MICHAEL JORDAN MISTAKE

Michael Jordan is the best basketball player ever. He led the NBA in scoring in 10 seasons as a professional player. He made the NBA's all-defensive first team 9 times. He has the highest total points scored in the playoffs in history, with 5,987. Those are only a few of his list of accomplishments on the court.

On October 6, 1993 Michael Jordan announced his retirement from professional basketball. On February 7, 1994, Jordan signed a contract with the Chicago White Sox and was assigned to their double-A minor league team, the Birmingham Barons. While Michael Jordan remains unsurpassed in basketball, it turns out that at baseball, he was just okay. He had a .202 batting average, hit 2 home runs, he had 51 runs batted in and 30 stolen bases. He could play baseball, but he wasn't a standout. Had it not been for the celebrity of his basketball career, he would have played largely without notice in

Birmingham.

The Michael Jordan mistake is trying to be good at everything. That we can be good at anything we choose, is a nice thought. The truth is we can get *better* at anything, but we can't be *good* at everything, so stop trying. You heard me - Stop trying!

That's not to say that Michael Jordan is only good at basketball, but this is what he is *famously successful* at doing. We can and should be famously successful at what we are best at. Granted, your level of fame may vary depending on your field of endeavor and the size of your sphere of influence. However, in some circle, you can and should be *famously successful* at what you do best. Everyone should, and everyone can, but not if you make the Michael Jordan mistake – trying to be good at everything.

7

3 MISTAKES
MISTAKE #2 – THE MARTY MCFLY MISTAKE

Remember the movie "Back to the Future" starring Michael J. Fox, as Marty Mcfly? In one scene when Jennifer, Marty's girlfriend, is trying to convince Marty to send his band's demo tape to a record producer, Marty replies, "What if I send it in and they don't like it? What if they say I'm no good? What if they say 'Get out of here, kid. You got no future?' I mean, I just don't think I can take that kind of rejection."

The Marty McFly Mistake is fixating on your weaknesses.

We do this all the time. We recognize an area where we seem to have no ability, no talent, and we fixate on it. We do this because we feel that we are somehow less than others who are good at what they do. We feel like we don't measure up. We compare ourselves to people we view as more successful and we tell ourselves we need to be more like them. Then we conclude that to be more like them we have to be good where they are good.

And not just good, but as good, or better than they are in that area. What we are really doing, is trying to be them.

There are two problems with this line of thinking. First, that person you are comparing yourself to, probably has one or more talents that help them be uniquely gifted in that area of endeavor. Second, and most importantly, when you fixate on your weaknesses by comparing yourself to others, you begin to disregard your own talents. This is when you start to disengage from your own talent development in favor of trying to develop skills in areas where others are talented.

That last point is key. You try to develop *skills* where others have *talent.* Skills can be learned. Talent is a part of you. It is in-born, a part of who you are. If you try to become better where you have no talent, the most you can hope to develop is some skill in that area. Meanwhile, the people, talented in that area, will continue to outperform you. For example, I can learn skills to become more analytical. I can learn to use tools for analysis and techniques for interpreting data. In contrast, someone with true talents for analysis will, by nature, see patterns in data. They will have an in-born ability to think of all the factors that might impact a situation based on the data. They will love to work with numbers and take deep dives into what they mean. The difference between someone like me who is not analytical, and someone who has a talent for analysis, is the person with analytical talent will love doing this stuff. I will simply perform it because my job requires it. The analytical person will be energized. I will be drained. The analytical person will thrive in analysis. I will get through it as quickly as possible so I can move on to something else. Another area where I have talent.

What we see in practice is something like this. I work with a peer who has a particular talent and a situation arises where they are able to really display their talent and shine. They receive recognition for it, are applauded and recognized. I see this recognition and see them being the hero and my ego starts to make me think that I'm not measuring up. I see situations in isolation and out of context and I begin to think I'm less valuable than my peer. I start to fixate on my weaknesses. I see that my peer, Andrea, who is strongly analytical is getting accolades for her work on a particular project or task. I didn't get the same recognition and so I tell myself, I need to be more like Andrea. I need to develop my analytical skills so that next time it can be me who gets the recognition. I fixate on what I can't do.

A better response would be to allow myself to celebrate Andrea in her moments of glory. She's got analytical talents, and she should be celebrated for pursuing and developing them to the point where she actually can outshine the rest of the team in that area. Rather than compare myself to Andrea and compete with Andrea, I need to look inward and understand the things that I do best – my talents. Because when Andrea does what she does best, and I do what I do best, we can help each other and be much better as a team, than we ever could be on our own.

In the end, even Marty McFly had his moment to shine with his guitar, but his real talent was in making things happen. He could turn thoughts and ideas into action. He got his "future" dad and mom, George and Lorainne, to kiss at the Enchantment Under the Sea dance so that they could fall in love, get married and restore things to the way they were supposed to be.

Don't make the Marty McFly Mistake. Don't fixate on your weaknesses. Focus on your strengths.

8

3 MISTAKES

MISTAKE #3 – THE CAITLYN JENNER MISTAKE

Born William Bruce Jenner, and crowned the "World's Greatest Athlete in 1976 as the winner of the Olympic Decathlon, in 2015 Bruce announced that he had struggled his entire life with gender identity. That same year, Bruce completed a gender transformation to become Caitlyn Jenner. According to Bruce, "The uncomfortableness of being me never leaves all day long." He then said of his gender transformation, "I'm not doing this to be interesting, I'm doing this to live." The Caitlyn Jenner Mistake is trying to be someone you're not based on others' expectations or dreams for you – living someone else's dream.

I call this the Caitlyn Jenner Mistake, realizing, who Bruce Jenner was, was not his choice and so was not a mistake he made. I use this as an extreme example to ilustrate that when we try to be someone we're not by living someone else's dream or expectation of us, we put ourselves in a very awkward and uncomfortable situation. Not unlike what Caitlyn Jenner describes. It's a very illustrative example. Like Caitlyn, you make the necessary changes "to live".

We see this all the time in more everyday examples, but the outcome is the same. We live someone else's dream for us. We might be trying to follow in someone else's shoes, like a parent or older sibling. It may even go on for generations. We hear people referred to as coming from a "long line" of doctors, or lawyers, or accountants, or entrepreneurs, or whatever. There's nothing wrong with that if you share similar talents and interests. The real tragedy comes, when you have other dreams for yourself, but continue the charade so as not to disappoint or upset those whose dreams you are pursuing.

Here's the bottom line on living someone else's dream, it's ridiculous.

That's right, and it's potentially, and probably, a waste of your talent. Even if it's a parent's chosen profession, it's not likely that you have the exact same talents for that profession. You may share some of those talents, but you are unique. All that aside, ask yourself, how did you end up where you are in your career or course for your life? Is it because it's what you wanted, or is it because of some external pressure? Did you get here because a parent, or a friend, or a teacher, or a religious leader or some other influential person suggested it? Suggestions are good, and can be helpful in guiding us along life's path, but in the end, did you arrive where you are because you chose to be here, or was it due to an unwillingness to disappoint someone else?

How do we see the Caitlyn Jenner Mistake in practice? To be very specific, let's say your father is an engineer. He's been very successful and enjoys his work. He loves Mondays. In his fervor and excitement about all things engineering and all of his accomplishments, he wants the same for his daughter. He wants her to be as happy and Monday-loving as he has always been because he loves her. He assumes, mistakenly, that if it worked for him it can work for you, his daughter (or son, don't get hung up on my gender selection, I'm trying to make a point here. Stay with me). He tells you that you should pursue engineering and influences you to do so all through high school and college. You graduate with an engineering degree and head out into the workforce. You have learned the skills and can do the job. You even have flashes of greatness and everything is going really well. Dad's proud, you're making money. Everything's good, except…you're miserable. This isn't what you wanted to do. It's what dad wanted for you. And now you're stuck, or think you are, anyway.

Don't make the Caitlyn Jenner Mistake. Don't live someone else's dream for you.

9

MY STORY
A PARTICULARLY HATEFUL MONDAY

February 17, 2014. I'm sitting at my desk, first floor, corner of the Fortune 500 Company where I've spent the last 20 years. It's about 8:30, the sun is shining through the window and I'm preparing for the scrum of the day. I have some meetings, some calls to clients to make, and some one on ones with members of the team that I manage. While I'm lining out my day, my cell phone rings and I can see it's my boss calling. I answer and I hear him ask if I'm in the office – an odd question for 8:30 on a Monday – but I reply, "Yes, I'm at my desk." I hear him say, "Can you meet me in the front lobby?" I respond with, "Sure, I'll be right there."

I end the call realizing I'm never coming back to that desk again. In 5 seconds I have reached a level of anxiety I've never experienced. My breathing is short and shallow. I look around the desk and wonder what I should take with me. Should I take my coat? Should I take my back pack. I regain my composure enough to realize that will look really stupid should I be wrong about the subject of this meeting.

I need to get going, he's waiting…they're waiting. Finally, I decide to take what I always take to meetings, my notebook, my pen, and my phone.

I stand. My knees are weak, breathing is difficult, but I make my way toward the lobby. I pass a few people and smile what must have seemed very nervous smiles, but I'm doing my best. It's difficult to talk or make any sound, really, so I just smile the nervous smiles and hope I can stop passing people. This is really hard.

I push the frosted glass door to the lobby, it's heavier than it's ever seemed before. I step into the lobby, the receptionist looks at me with a grim look of recognition. She knows what's going on as there are several of us having these meetings today. She just doesn't know who until she sees each one of us come through the door.

I look left and through the frosted glass of the conference room I see the image of my boss and someone else. That confirms my suspicion. This is it.

I walk into the room my boss greets me and introduces someone from HR who I don't know, have never seen. In an instant she becomes nameless and faceless. At a moment like this my brain is not taking on information it will never use again.

I sit down and my boss tells me, "As you are aware, we are going through a reorganization, and today is your last day here." I'm given particulars and about 5 minutes later, I'm back out into the lobby where I spend a few more minutes with an outplacement person who I also don't know and have never seen before. Another person my brain refuses to remember.

I get a few more details, during which my coat and backpack are delivered to me, and I'm ushered through the front door to make my way around to the back of the building to where my car is. As I walk I wonder if people are watching me wondering why I'm walking around to my car so early in the morning. It's awkward. I want to get away from here. I want to get in my car and get far away. I don't want to talk to my family. I don't want to talk to anyone. I want to run. This job has defined me for so much of my life. It's required so much of my time and energy. It was who I am…who I was. Now what?

That was a very bad Monday indeed. My worst ever. But, it was preceded by a couple of hundred bad Mondays. Not this bad, but bad in their own right.

You see, I'd spent about 4 years hating Mondays. Part of the 70%. Some Mondays were worse than others, but all were pretty bad. All of them started for me around 6 o'clock on Sunday evening and dragged on until Monday evening. Ironically, I wasn't getting paid on Sunday night, but I was still giving my time and energy to the organization.

So why did I hate Mondays for 4 years? And why didn't I do anything about it? Those are two very good questions and with hindsight, I will explain the answers.

Why did I go on hating mondays for so long? Jump back even further in time. Maybe 6 years prior to February 17, 2014. Jump back to 2008. At that time I was in a job I really enjoyed. It wasn't perfect. There were struggles, but I was able to be me – to use my personality and talents to do what I do best.

However, I was starting to feel the pressure to move to the next level of management. Let me be clear, no one was applying this pressure. It was self-imposed by my thinking that people were starting to think I should be moving further in my career. This is a version of the Caitlyn Jenner Mistake. The truth is I was never that interesting. No one was up at night worrying about my career progression but me. But for me it became an incessant preoccupation. I'd been a manager for many years and felt I was stagnating. I was only looking at the position and failing to see what I was accomplishing. I really was making progress though my title stayed the same. This is an important point that everyone should realize. Your title has very little to do with what you are learning and the degree of your success. But my ego said it was time for a bigger title. And so I pursued every opportunity to get that bigger title. At every attempt, I was disappointed. I started to resent the situation and started to really play the victim. Part of the problem, was that I lived in Salt Lake City, and though I managed a team at the headquarters in Atlanta remotely, I really needed to be in Atlanta to be effective as a member of the senior team. I was encouraged to seek opportunities in a different business unit, in Salt Lake where I live.

Still thinking that I needed to move to a higher position to make career progress, I took a lateral position just to get into the local business unit. The hope was to make an impact and then be considered for advancement opportunities there. I found out early, that this new role was a bad fit for me.

I didn't enjoy the work and though I was still managing people, the vision and values in this new organization were different than mine. I tried to morph, and twist to try to conform, to be more like my peers who had established their careers in this environment. I could see them being successful and so I tried to do what they did, and be like them. That's a problem. I wasn't like them. They weren't even like each other. So there was no magic formula, and the more I tried to be this amalgam of the best I saw in all of them, the more I buried my own unique talents. The talents that had made me successful for so many years, all this so I could fit into this new business unit. The more time I spent in this part of the organization, the more square a peg I seemed to become. Feedback I would get was completely different than what I had ever received before. I tried to incorporate that feedback, but the harder I tried, the more my personality and talents got shoehorned into a small box the corner of who I am, and the more ineffective I became. I kept trying to be everything I was not. The Michael Jordan Mistake.

I was not being successful at all. I had a highly engaged team, but that's always been fairly automatic for me. However, some of the measures I'd been so good at achieving in my old job seemed unattainable to me now, and I couldn't seem to figure out why.

Looking back I can see it clearly now. First, I started by telling myself I needed a higher position, but I really didn't want that. Again, this is a version of the Caitlyn Jenner Mistake. I was trying to live someone else's dream or expectation for me. It was actually just my perception of what others' expectations were. Moving to a higher position would mean I would be more removed from the front-line people I loved to help develop – my true passion. I would have to be more strategic, but I don't have talent for that. I have talent for developing people – the thing that I do best. Executive level requirements and priorities are different. So even in my old business unit, I was probably not going to be a good fit for an executive level position, because my talents were not suited for that role.

Next, being unsatisfied in the position that was such a good fit for me, I moved to a part of the organization where the values were not aligned with mine and I had to start changing to align with theirs, but that's really not possible. Not for anyone, in any organization. We value what we value. Our values are not situational, and if we try to pretend they are, we engage in a text book example of cognitive dissonance – having inconsistent thoughts, beliefs or attitudes related to behavioral decisions.

Then, I kept trying hard to do the things the way others did them. I compared myself and competed with my peers, trying to duplicate what they did the way they did them. Because I didn't think I could take the rejection I might face if I didn't try to fix my weaknesses – The Marty McFly Mistake. I buried my talents and tried to skill my way through it. I failed most of the time. This was a bad job fit and no matter how long I stuck with it, no matter how hard I tried to do everything right, I was never going to fit in or be successful. You can't turn your weaknesses into strengths. It is NOT possible! You can make them lesser weaknesses, but you will never be strong where you don't have talent. What's more, the opportunity cost of giving up on the development of your in-born talents is *immense.*

Ironically, at the time I was fired, I couldn't believe it. How could they let *me* go? I'm not the lowest performer, what's going on? The answer is that there are a lot of factors, and though I may not have been the lowest performer, it was clear, probably clearer to them than to me, that this was a bad fit and the best thing for me was to get out of there. I'm grateful that they saw fit to do something I was unlikely and unwilling to do on my own, get rid of me. It took me less than 24 hours to see I was already happier, and I was unemployed! What's more, now the world was wide open. I had at least another 20 years of career ahead of me. Now it was up to me to determine how I would do what I do best every day. Today, I do what I do best EVERY day. I get up around 5 o'clock every morning excited about the day, even MONDAYS! I love Monday, just like Friday, but for a different reason.

What about you? Do you hate Mondays? Are you struggling with a bad job fit? When you look back at your life so far, are you who you thought you'd be?

ARE YOU WHO YOU THOUGHT YOU'D BE?

"I'm not who I thought I was. I'm not. And I'm terrified that I never will be." This is a sentiment expressed in desperation by Rory Jansen, a character played by Bradley Cooper in the movie "The Words". In the movie, Rory Jansen is a frustrated and struggling novelist who stumbles upon another writer's long, lost and magnificent manuscript. In the moment he expresses this fear, he's just read the manuscript and realizes he doesn't have that sort of talent in him. He wonders if he's been wasting his time.

This is a sentiment that crosses a lot of minds. For some it's during a mid-life moment of reflection. For others it hits every Sunday afternoon as we look down the barrel of another stressful and frustrating work week.

Has a similar sentiment crossed your mind? Is it in your mind now? Maybe the words are different. Maybe they come in form of a question. "What am I doing here?" "Why do I keep doing this?" "How did I get here? When I was 20 I didn't think this was where I was headed."

Maybe your parents influenced you. Maybe you fell into what you thought was an opportunity that didn't pan out. Maybe you did the "responsible" thing and took the safe job that would pay the bills. But now you're unhappy and wondering what to do about it.

This is where you go before you develop a passion for Monday. I'm assuming because you're reading this little book that this is where you are now – with at best a distaste for Monday, at worst an anxious fear of them.

It's time to take back your Mondays – and with them, probably the last half of every weekend for the rest of your life. But how do you do that? You start with your talents. When we talk about talent, most people go to things like music or painting of some other visual or performing art. Those are evidence of talent, but did you know that there are other talents that at least at the outset may sound more mundane. Be that as it may they are still talents. I'll give you a few hints at some things that indicate talent.

- You strike up a conversation with people in the line at the store, next to you on a bus, or wherever you go.
- You see patterns in sets of data on screen or a printed page.
- You are the one that tends to put on the brakes during conversations about process changes or implementing a new service.
- You love talking. You love words. You love stories. You love to tell people about things you know.
- You collect all sorts of information.

You can't seem to get enough. You can spend time surfing the web from one point to the next just gathering data that you file away in your brain with the intent to use it in a time of need, or to help others.

- You would rather start a project than talk about it. You get something in your mind and you just can't wait to get going on it. You might even start before it's fully planned out.
- You somehow just know in any situation what people should be doing. You can take quick stock of the situation and know what everyone in the room should do.

Do those sound like talents to you, or do they just sound like living. Here's one more clue, if any of them sound just like living to you, it's likely because you have the talent that is behind those behaviors and actions. The ones that sound a little crazy, a little out there, a little like, "Who would do that?" – those are the ones you probably don't have as dominant talents.

Believe it or not, these are talents. They are parts of 34 talent themes found to be universal in all people, but appearing in different degrees in individuals. A man named Dr. Donald O. Clifton dedicated his life and career to finding out what made people who were successful, so successful. His work began in the 1950s and culminated nearly a half-century later after exhaustive research and testing. He developed a tool to determine how these 34 talent themes rank in individuals. For example, do you have Analytical talents in your top 5 or in 34th place? The tool is called the Clifton StrengthsFinder. It's an assessment of talent based on your answers to 177 questions. There's a lot more to it than I will explain here, in fact it's got its own book, StrengthsFinder 2.0 that will explain it far better. The bottom line is, it's the best way to determine what your individual talent themes are. It gives you either your top 5 talent themes, you can obtain all 34, but the top 5 are plenty to chew on. The results are unique to only you. The chances of you finding someone else with your same top 5 talent themes, in the same order, is 1 in 33 million. It's incredibly useful information. But talent is over-rated, right?

There is a popular notion that talent, though nice to have, is over-rated. There's a whole field of study and research around this.

The concept is that you can become world-class at any endeavor. You just have to put in 10,000 hours of deliberate practice with coaching and professional supervision. Only 10,000 hours! That's just 4.8 years at 40 hours per week. So if you want to be a professional golfer, or a world-class pianist, you *can* get there. The theory is that everyone who is great at anything did just that. Most of them started early in life, so it was less disruptive than say, taking up baseball in your mid-30s, but in theory, you *could* do that. The question is, *should* you?

What is ignored when following this line of thinking is the opportunity cost of unplugging from the things you're good at, while you plug-in to the 10,000 hours of deliberate practice. All development in areas where you true talents lie, will necessarily cease. You won't have time to work on your talents. You'll need to devote all your waking time to the pursuit of something you're probably no good at doing.

The other thing that is ignored is any deference to true in-born talent. Put plainly, what happens if you decide you want to be a professional basketball player or a pop star and you start at the same time with your practice as Michael Jordan or Taylor Swift?

Do you really think you will end up being Michael Jordan's nemesis or writing recording and performing as many hits as Taylor Swift?

How about a real-life example? Let's go back to Michael Jordan, not for a mistake this time. I'm roughly the same age as Michael Jordan. Growing up in the 70s and 80s in Utah, I had aspirations of playing basketball with the Utah Jazz – be the hometown hero. I put in hours and hours of very deliberate practice. I was serious about this. I wasn't practicing trick shots and fancy ball handling. I practiced for hours and hours on drills. I worked on left-handed lay ups and rebounding. I practiced for hours dribbling with my left, non-dominant hand. I spent hours running the school playground dribbling around rocks, and poles and other imagined defenders. When the cold Utah winters set in, I would shovel the driveway so that I could still play and I would play beyond the point where my fingers were sore. They were numb with skin cracking, but I still played until it got too dark to see. I have no way of knowing, but I believe I spent a similar amount of time on the practice court as Michael Jordan.

Now let's look at where Michael and I ended up.

Michael Jordan became the best basketball player ever. 6 championships, 5-time MVP, most seasons leading the league in scoring (his rookie year was one of these), two gold medals, and the basketball hall of fame. Though some of his records are falling, players like LeBron James and Kobe Bryant will always have as their number one goal - *to catch up to Michael Jordan.*

So what about me? I put in all those hours, where did my basketball career take me? I didn't make the high school team. So my career came to a premature end. Premature in my eyes, but to the rest of the world, I ended up about where I should be in the annals of basketball history. Interestingly, that doesn't upset me. It's not where my talents lie. And now that I've discovered my talents I spend exactly zero hours per day playing basketball. I just didn't have the combination of talents necessary to be a world class basketball player. I realize that probably didn't make it to 10,000 hours of practice, and who knows where I'd be if I had. I'm pretty sure I put in more hours than some of the kids who *did* make my high school team. Talent is the difference. Talent is far from over-rated.

I don't have to be good at everything. I have other talents to offer the world. I can be the best at what I'm good at, even famously successful in my corner of the world, and that's good enough for me. Should I ever have the need for a behind the back slam dunk, I'll go find someone with a talent for basketball to do one for me. I hope I'll be able to help that person, with the talents I have and we'll both be better off.

10

PLAY TO YOUR STRENGTHS
AVOIDING THE MICHAEL JORDAN MISTAKE

Play to your strengths! We hear people say it. We read about in in articles in magazines and hear about it on TV. But, do we believe it? Do we believe we should really focus on what we do best at the potential expense of turning our weaknesses in to strengths? As a society do we believe we should focus on our strengths? Look around you. Do you see people around you doing what they do best almost to the exclusion of what they do worst?

Do your parents believe you should play to your strengths? Did mom and dad tell you to pursue that dream of being a writer, or actor or garbage collector? Or did they say, "You'll never make money doing that. What you should do is…"

Did your schools believe it? Did you have a guidance counselor or teacher say, "That's okay, Billy. You don't have to focus on math. Your strengths is in art, so let's have you perfect your artistic talents."

Do your friends believe it? Are they playing to their strengths? Have they pursued their dreams and what they do best, or in the end, did they fall into the same sensibility argument that your parents pulled on you?

Most importantly, do *you* believe it? Do you believe you should play to your strengths? Do you believe that time spent on your strengths and how to use them will bring you more success and satisfaction than focusing on your weaknesses?

It's no wonder we don't believe it. Given our background, upbringing and the focus of society, it's no wonder we don't believe we should focus on our strengths. And it's not just what we hear during our formative years. Consider an example – the annual review with your boss. Your boss brings you into her office, sits you down across the desk and reviews the highs, the lows, the ins, the outs, the ups, the downs, and everything in between, thanks you for hard work, praises you for your strengths and then says…"Here are your areas of opportunity." Better, and more honestly known as your weaknesses. We hate weaknesses so bad, that we even had to make up a goofy name for them. Your boss then proceeds to help you develop goals to improve your "areas of opportunity."

We then embark on another year of frustration trying to become "well-rounded". And we tell ourselves that we want to do this. We strive to become better in our areas of weakness. Because weaknesses are bad, right? Our weaknesses make us feel "less than", right? And we can't feel bad, or less than, because life is a competition, right?

What if rather than viewing life as a competition, we looked at it as a big collaboration? What if rather than comparing myself to you, and competing with you, and telling myself, I like what you do, I should be more like you… what if instead, I tried to be the best possible *me* I can be? What if I focus on my strengths? That way you be the best at what you're good at, I become the best at what I'm good at, and then we collaborate and are both much better together than we can be on our own. In Economics, this is referred to as specialization and exchange. The point being, if I'm really good at making clothing and you're really good at making food, in our tiny economy of two people, I can make you really good clothing and I'll exchange my really good clothing for your really good food. The alternative is that I'm a well-dressed eater of leaves and dirt and anything else I can find, while you are well-fed but dressed in leaves and dirt and anything else *you* can find.

The point is, you do what you do really well, I do what I do really well, we share the product of our really great and talent-driven efforts and we're both better off than we could ever be on our own.

11

STOP TRYING TO BE WELL-ROUNDED

AVOIDING THE MARTY MCFLY MISTAKE

But you have to be good at everything! You have to be everything to everyone because if you do that, you have the greatest shot at popularity, you'll be in greater demand and you can leave a bigger mark on the world, right? Wrong.

If you try to be really good at everything, you'll end up being really great at nothing.

In an interview with Piers Morgan on CNN, Oprah Winfrey said, "One of the things I admire about myself is, I know where my lane is, and I know how to stay in my lane." Oprah knows her strengths. She knows what to do to continue on her course of doing what she does best, and she's successful – *famously successful.*

Look at anyone who is famously successful, and you'll find that the common element is that they focus on their strengths. They know, like Oprah, how to stay in their lane. Oprah, Steve Jobs, Taylor Swift, Michael

Jordan, they all have found their area of excellence and within that larger area they have developed their greatest talents to the point that they are famously successful – perhaps the most famous, and most successful in their respective fields.

Taylor Swift, we know her as a singer, but within that discipline, she is a song writer as well and she is so successful that virtually everyone else even in her industry are chasing her. But what if she said, I also want to be a producer, design the cover art, schedule my own interviews, arrange my own travel, produce my own concerts… that's enough distraction that she might still be producing her first album, rather than touring in support of her 5th.

As much as you've heard about the value of being well rounded, I'm going to try and change your mind about that. I'm going to convince you to find out what your top talents are, and then focus on developing them into strengths. Because you should be a star, just like Taylor Swift, just like Michael Jordan, just like Oprah. You will form teams of other stars with whom you can collaborate, and in those teams you'll be well-rounded, together. Taylor Swift does what she does best – writing songs and singing. Her band members do what they do best – being among the best players in the industry. Her producer does what he does best - putting all the tracks and sounds together into a catchy composition that sounds great. The finished product is Taylor Swift. And though we may only see her, or think of her when we hear her music, without a team of people doing what they do best, Taylor, as talented as she is, could not achieve as much alone as she does with her team.

Let's look at another, perhaps more vivid example. Who's Ted Sorensen? Not ringing a bell?

John F. Kennedy said in his inaugural address:

"Ask not what your country can do for you. Ask what you can do for your country." While it is true JFK said this, Ted Sorensen wrote it. Ted Sorensen wrote a lot of other speeches for JFK. He also was one of his chief strategists. JFK said of Ted Sorensen that he was his "Intellectual blood bank" and an "indispensable member of my team". There are some who question whether or not JFK would have been elected President had it not been for Ted Sorensen.

But did Ted Sorensen say, "I wrote the speeches, I got you here. I should be president!" No, he didn't. Ted Sorensen knew his lane and he knew how to stay in his lane. He had an important role and it was the role that supported and fed his talents and therefore, he loved his job, and he was good at it – among the best ever in his role and famously successful within his circle.

It's the same concept for all of us. You don't have to compete with, compare yourself to, and try and be someone else. Instead, you should discover your strengths and be the best you can be where your talents lie. Then you can collaborate with others who are the best at what they do. Together you can be outstanding and well-rounded as a team.

12

DON'T LIVE SOMEONE ELSE'S DREAM

AVOIDING THE CAITLYN JENNER MISTAKE

Are you doing the safe thing? Are you doing the sensible thing? Are you living the dream of your parents? Even if you can't identify with Caitlyn Jenner, the concept probably resonates on some level. Have you ever been to a little league game where a dad is taking the whole thing a little too seriously? Or have you ever heard of toddler beauty pageants, where mothers dress their daughters up like pageant queens from the time they are barely old enough to walk? Venues like these are where living someone else's dream starts. Later in life, during teenage or college years, well-intended parents may point us toward a career they have or wish they had. In other cases, parents or other influencers may direct you to a finite list of careers – the ones they know about and that seem like they will provide a stable living.

The problem is that in these situations, there is little regard paid to what your interests are or what your talents might dictate. And so, we settle for sensible. We have to pay the rent, buy food, make the care payment, so get a good job that will allow for these things.

I hear of people all the time who follow the career path they think will make others' happy. What they find out at some point is, they either have to settle for Monday's they hate, or retrain and finally pursue their own dreams. I know of a man who started his career as a very successful Electrical Engineer. He progressed to influential positions in his company. Then, around age 40, he decided that his true passion was for medicine. He went back to school to become a doctor and that's what he's doing today. The good news from this example, is that it's never too late. Most of us will not have to go through 8 more years of school at middle age to play to our strengths.

13

FINDING A PASSION FOR MONDAY

So now what do you do? You agree, you're part of the 70% that hate Mondays, but what's next. Now you have to do something about it. Something that will help you LOVE Monday, just like Friday, but for a different reason.

I use an acronym that provides an easy association for remembering the formula. I call it the LOVE Monday's Formula. It's based on the word LOVE as an acronym.

L - IS FOR LEARN!

Learn about your strengths. Discover them and learn all you can about your top talent themes. The easiest way to do this is to take the Clifton StrengthsFinder assessment of talent. As mentioned earlier, this is a scientifically sound and proven tool to help you learn about your top talents. You can purchase the best-selling book, StrengthsFinder 2.0, by Tom Rath. You can also log on to GallupStrengthsCenter.com and take the assessment there.

O - IS FOR OBSERVE!

Observe people who are famously successful in their fields of endeavor. I have touched on this a couple of times in this book already. I want to reiterate that anyone and everyone who is famously successful at what they do, plays to their strengths and not their weaknesses. They don't ignore their weaknesses, but they find someone or something to help them in their weak areas so that they don't lose precious time and waste scarce energy on them.

V - IS FOR VISUALIZE!

Look out onto the horizon – a year, two years, five years. Visualize yourself being famously successful at what you do best. Once you find out what your true, in-born talents are, you will want to use them every day. As you focus on using your talents, they will transform into strengths.

E - IS FOR ENERGIZE!

Working in your strengths is very energizing. People who work in their strengths report that time passes without notice and when their work period ends, they can't wait to get back to working in their strengths again. You may be able to use your strengths in your current role. If not, with proper focus and coaching, you can find a career in an organization where you can spend hours every day doing what you do best.

WHERE DO I BEGIN?

Mark Twain said, "the two most important days of your life are the day you were born, and the day you find out why." Some call it mission, some call it passion, whatever you call it, do you know what it is for you? Have you discovered why you were born?

As a manager in a Fortune 500 Corporation for nearly 20 years, I interviewed hundreds of people. A question I often asked during these interview was:

"Tell me about a job, project or task you've had where time passed without notice, where you felt 'in the flow' and when you felt more energized at the end of

the day than you did at the beginning?"

I asked this recently to a woman who was feeling like she had a job like that many years ago. The term she used to describe that time was that she was "rockin' it". However you describe it, rockin' it, flow, or any other descriptive term, you know what it's like. You're not watching the clock, you have lots of energy, you learn quickly and easily and you can't wait to do it again. These are all signs of working with your strengths. You know it when you're doing it because you feel it, and the feeling is undeniable. Conversely, you know when you're not working with your strengths because you feel that as well. If you feel drained at the end of the day physically, emotionally and spiritually, you probably didn't get to use your strengths much that day. Also, if time was dragging and you found yourself easily distracted, you probably weren't using your strengths during that time.

Another example is a time when you were truly happy at work? What was going on? What were you doing? What were your interactions with people like?

The point is, you can't be in the flow or happy or energetic when you are not using your strengths. If you seldom find yourself in the flow, happy or energetic, then best case, you're not playing to your strengths in your current role – this can be fixed. Worst case, you are in the wrong job all together – this can also be fixed, but it's a bigger step, so let's be sure about it.

WHEN WERE YOU IN THE FLOW?

Let's take a minute to contemplate this flow/energetic/happy state. Either in the book or on a separate sheet, answer the following questions:

1. In what occupation, project or task did I feel in the flow, filled with energy, and the time passed almost without notice?

   ____

   _____.

2. Describe a typical day for you in this role

   ____

   ____

   ____

   ____

   ____

   ____

   ____

   ____

   ____

   ____

   ____

   ____

   ____

3. What were the tasks in this role that gave you energy? What tasks did you enjoy the most?

4. What kinds of things do you learn quickly and easily? If you're having trouble think back to that time you were in the flow.

5. Describe any moments when you did something really well and wondered, "How did I do that?"

6. How often do you get to do these tasks or similar tasks in your current role (daily, weekly, monthly, etc.)?

   ____

   ____

7. What proportion of your time each day or each week do you spend in these most loved tasks in your current role (Circle one)?
   5% 10% 25% 50% >50%

What Can You Do to Have a Passion for Monday?

1. Let's go back to that role you defined from your past where you felt you were in the flow, energetic, you learned things quickly and time passed without notice.
2. Now answer these questions:
3. Does a role that allows you to play to your strengths exist where you work?

   ____

4. What are those roles?

   ____

   ____

   ____

   ____

   ____

   ____

5. Do you meet the minimum requirements for any of these roles?

6. Would you be willing to talk to your manager about this?

7. If yes, what do you hope the outcome will be?

When you talk to your manager, speak to him or her in terms of your strengths. The more you can define these definitively, the better. Again a good place to start is by taking the Clifton StrengthsFinder assessment at GallupStrengthsCenter.com. Once you know your top strengths you can speak in terms of what you do best, using examples from your past. You can also speak about your aspirations and how you intend to use your strengths to propel yourself in that direction.

CONCLUSION

You really can shed your contempt for Monday. You have to stop making the 3 mistakes that make people hate Monday. You need to learn about and develop your strongest talents. You need to observe people who are famously successful in their areas of excellence and draw upon what they do to play to their strengths. You need to visualize yourself in that future state where you are doing what you do best every day. Finally, you need to start working with your talents each day, even in small ways, so that you can derive the energy you need to lift you yet higher.

The reason I love Mondays, and every

other day of the week, is that I get to do what I do best every day. I spend my days working with people both individually and in organizations to discover and do what they do best every day. If you're not there, you can get there. If you're not sure how, find me at Qwerke.com. Together we'll get you and your organization doing what you do best every day too.

You can really can LOVE Monday, just like Friday, but for a different reason. That's what gaining a passion for Monday is all about.

SOURCES

"State of the American Workplace." *Gallup.com*. N.p., n.d. Web. 18 Sept. 2015.

Buckingham, Marcus, and Curt Coffman. First, Break All the Rules: What the World's Greatest Managers Do Differently. New York, NY.: Simon & Schuster, 1999.

"STRESS...At Work." *Centers for Disease Control and Prevention*. Centers for Disease Control and Prevention, 06 June 2014. Web. 20 Oct. 2015.

"Piers Morgan Tonight - Oprah Winfrey." *.com*. N.p., n.d. Web. 21 Oct. 2015

"Gallup Employee Engagement Center." *Gallup Q12 Employee Engagement Center*. N.p., n.d. Web. 14 Oct. 2015.

Gallup Managing for Engagement Resource Kit. Gallup.

"Back to the Future." *IMDb*. IMDb.com, n.d. Web. 10 Oct. 2015.

"Michael Jordan." *Wikipedia*. Wikimedia Foundation, n.d. Web. 15 Oct. 2015.

"Caitlyn Jenner." *Wikipedia*. Wikimedia Foundation, n.d. Web. 15 Oct. 2015.

"Caitlyn Jenner." *Caitlyn Jenner*. N.p., n.d. Web. 15 Oct. 2015.

"The Words." *IMDb*. IMDb.com, n.d. Web. 08 Oct. 2015.

Colvin, Geoffrey. *Talent Is Overrated: What Really Separates World-class Performers from Everybody Else*. New York: Portfolio, 2008. 82. Print.

Bissinger, Buzz. "Caitlyn Jenner: The Full Story." Vanity Fair. N.p., n.d. Web. 02 Nov. 2015.

Asplund, Jim, Shane J. Lopez, Tim Hodges, and Jim Harter. "Clifton StrengthsFinder 2.0 Technical Report." *The Clifton StrengthsFinder ® 2.0* (2007): n. pag. *Gallup.Strengths.Com*. Gallup. Web. 15 Oct. 2015.

THE AUTHOR

Ryan Houmand is Co-founder and CEO at Qwerke. He transforms good managers into superb managers and builds the world's most engaged teams. Since his first job as the manager of a snow cone stand in Port Arthur, Texas he has been in leadership. He spent nearly 20 years as a manager in a Fortune 500 corporation. He has a passion for making the world of work a better place to be. He holds a bachelor's degree in Economics from Brigham Young University and an MBA from the University of Phoenix. He is a Gallup-Certified Strengths Coach. Ryan gets to do what he does best every day at Qwerke, keynote speaking, and as a part-time snowboard instructor. Ryan's Top 5 strengths – Arranger, Activator, Positivity, Maximizer and Belief.

Ryan lives with his wife Jenn Loomis near Salt Lake City. Between them they have the 4 smartest, best-looking kids in the world and the 2 most mischievous dogs.

25657090R00048

Made in the USA
San Bernardino, CA
06 November 2015